T0243653

RACHEL MENNIES, SERIES EDITOR

Also in the series:

A DREAM IN WHICH I AM PLAYING WITH BEES

POEMS

RK FAUTH

TEXAS TECH UNIVERSITY PRESS

This book is typeset in Adobe Caslon Pro. The paper used in this book meets the minimum requirements of ANSI/NISO Z39.48-1992 (R1997). ♾

Designed by Hannah Gaskamp
Cover design by Hannah Gaskamp

Library of Congress Cataloging-in-Publication Data

Names: Fauth, RK, 1993– author. Title: A Dream in Which I Am Playing with Bees: Poems / RK Fauth. Description: Lubbock, Texas: Texas Tech University Press, 2024. |
Series: Walt McDonald First-Book Prize in Poetry | Summary: "A collection of poems made of natural imagery, queer metaphors, personal observations, and historical circumstances surrounding honeybees"—Provided by publisher.
Identifiers: LCCN 2023028024 | ISBN 978-1-68283-196-0 (cloth)
Subjects: LCGFT: Poetry
Classification: LCC PS3606.A876 D74 2024 | DDC 811/.6—dc23/eng/20230621
LC record available at https://lccn.loc.gov/2023028024

Printed in the United States of America
24 25 26 27 28 29 30 31 32 / 9 8 7 6 5 4 3 2 1

Texas Tech University Press
Box 41037
Lubbock, Texas 79409-1037 USA
800.832.4042
ttup@ttu.edu
www.ttupress.org

For LJ,
my planet

CONTENTS

CONTENTS

FAUNA

TERRA

ETHOS

FOREWORD

Behold, the earliest evidence of sweetness . . .

At the outset of RK Fauth's staggeringly bright debut collection, *A Dream in Which I Am Playing with Bees*, we're looking in every direction at once. Fauth points our gaze toward a simultaneous past-and-future "hindsight," as she names it in her introduction: a future-become-past where the bees are gone. Or, more precisely, to a moment when humanity has extinguished the bee, but also to the moment beyond extinction, and also before it, all in the same collection.

These poems do not exist solely to mourn or indict the loss of this vital ecologic wonder; in the collection, Fauth also raises the question of what's at stake for losing the bee from our very *language*, our ability to make metaphors from and tell stories about this creature and all it keeps alive for us through its labor. "What could disappear from our minds, our fantasies, and our self-descriptors," she asks, "if nature is no longer a mirror?"

What will the poets have left to say without the bees—without their pollinated fruit and their flowers, my own beloved vehicle in metaphor-making? Fauth builds this theoretical world alongside our own deftly and devastatingly in *A Dream in Which I Am Playing with Bees*, a collection that I'm honored to share with you as the most recent winner of the Walt McDonald First-Book Prize in Poetry.

As we follow the bee and all it reaps and sows throughout the collection, we first encounter a being whose labor bestows a fertilized lushness to the world— and whose work-products, like honey and royal jelly, have enriched humanity for millennia. We've come to depend on the bees, but we don't consider them often. Perhaps we don't consider them enough. One example of this often-overlooked productivity is propolis, a material bees make from certain trees to use in the creation of their hives that holds many uses for humans, as Fauth mines in

"Propolis: gummy, made for sealing crevices":

Propolis: gummy, made for sealing crevices
and old as honey . . .

Gynecological. Pliable. Cement.
For the larynx,
for treat. Meant for
burns and ulcers . . .

In the world before the bees have gone, the world we currently know and understand and remember, we look to the bees not only for their honey but for their housing and their healing—for our own designs. (Even today: peruse a skin-care counter and you'll find numerous propolis-infused serums and creams.) Fauth flips over this examination in "Propolis: rubbed from spiked thighs, bounded into wax" to reveal another key human (and animal, and insect) use for propolis:

caskets for tiny lizards, beetles who made the wrong turn, and
other invaders, spun by bees in a funeral garb called propolis.
To smother out germs, rival breath, moisture and
light.

The Egyptians knew. Propolis was our first embalmer.

Fomenter of life and protector in death, the bee inflects and stewards each stage of human existence—I immediately think of the flowers we catch at weddings and send after funerals. Bee labor shapes our rituals; it feeds and nourishes our bodies. As Fauth shows, it has even protected our dead.

It's tempting to find a moralizing lesson in the gaze Fauth casts on this all-important ecological figure: to confuse her focus solely with a fixed stare exhorting us to Do Something, lest her premonition come true. But Fauth resists this as a place to rest her attention, moving us between the stakes of a bee-less ecology and an imagined world where the bee exits not only our *ecosystem* but our *language*.

If the bees go, those born into a world without them—who will, theoretically, know nothing of honey or flowers or all else the bee fosters, as well as nothing of the creature itself—will also lose an entire poetic lexicon. Love can no longer be sweet like honey, a red-red rose; its loss cannot sting us and swell us with its venom.

In considering how nature and language tangle and construct one another, Fauth again resists simplistic lament or exhortation through her bee-lens. Instead, her speaker takes us to lush Appalachia in the collection's final moments, where queerness must code-switch to survive and love blooms, sweetly, in at-times hostile terrain. "A few weeks ago, the neighbor called out, *y'all sisters?* and we obviously said yes," the speaker notes in the poem "These Days We Imagine Getting a Gun." Appalachia is the birthplace of the speaker's partner, but an adopted home to the speaker, who learns the place's history through the lens of her beloved's memories.

In Appalachia, the bee and its fragrant co-creations adorn the speaker and her partner as they navigate this complicated landscape, as in the poem "Little Boy, There Are No Roses in This Poem" (one of my favorites in the collection—and this is no easy declaration). The speaker recalls an as-told memory of her partner, who is genderqueer, stealing peaches from a neighbor as a child:

You were hopping fences in Kentucky.
And he was a furious gardener. But also
the first stranger to ever call you the right thing, as in—
a boy. As if—that was all it took

to be seen:
sneak into the wrong yard, at the wrong biological time,
at the right distance, and just try, try,
to steal for yourself the juicy world
of a peach.

Even the act of pollination itself, as Fauth shows us in "The Botanical Tradition," is queer. "No male bee ever meets a flower, / let alone kisses her," the speaker tells us. "This is a pair of wives. . . . They love so good, the arrangement lives for eons, feeding itself."

The act of pollination, this abundance of nourishment, desire, and—vitally— sustainability, is named as queer intimacy. Such an approach opens the door for the possibility of the speaker's home-creation and love-fostering in this new and uncertain place. This act of naming marks yet another deft maneuver of Fauth's lyric examination of the bee in *A Dream in Which I Am Playing with Bees*. Here, we come to understand, through the language we need to describe this specific queer love in this specific place, the enormous stakes of what we'd lose in the bee's absence: both the love and the place, at once.

RACHEL MENNIES

A DREAM IN WHICH I AM PLAYING WITH BEES

INTRODUCTION

A Dream in Which I Am Playing with Bees is a collection of poems made of natural imagery, queer metaphors, personal observations, and historical circumstances surrounding honeybees. In the aftermath of a fictional bee extinction, I present these poems to the post-bee reader as "artifacts." These are poems in hindsight.

Whether in a line or an entire premise, none of the poems could think, speak, or see in the same way if bees—and the relations they make possible—suddenly disappeared. I've positioned *Playing with Bees* as poetry in hindsight to contemplate poetry's "natural" inclinations towards building alternative worlds through earthbound metaphors. Because, like any natural resource, the bee is a wellspring of possibility: essential, fragile, causal. And like any animal, the pollinating bee has enabled a diverse phylum of phrases and myths that humans trade to express our most hard-to-name feelings. But what happens to our creative faculties, or language in general, after a peg in the environment is removed?

This collection is not a "save the bees" work. That would be excellent, but I would be lying if I said I knew much about the science of bee conservation. In fact, the questions I'm asking are not necessarily bee-specific. I'm most interested in this: What could disappear from our minds, our fantasies, and our self-descriptors, if nature is no longer a mirror?

Consider an apocalypse in reverse. As artifacts, these poems are the residue of a dead species. But they are also the living offshoots of a playful, delicate landscape. *Playing with Bees* covets what's left. At the bottom of everything, we find the long-lost fragments of an ecologically intact dream.

PRELUDE

So the world turned
its one good eye

to watch the bees
take most of metaphor
                with them.

            Swarms—
                in all their airborne
            pointillism—
                        shifted on the breeze

for the last time. Of course,

the absence of bees
                        left behind significant
                                        holes
in our ecology. Less

                        obvious
            were the indelible holes
in poems, which would come
later:

Our vast psychic habitat
shrunk. Nothing was
            like nectar
                    of the gods

Nobody was warned by
a deep black dahlia, and nobody

grew like
            a weed.

Nobody felt spry as
            a daisy, or blue
            and princely

5

as a hyacinth; was lucid
     as a moon flower.   Nobody came home

      and yelled   *honey!* up the stairs,

And nothing in particular

by any other name would smell as sweet as—

Consider:
the verbal dearth
that is always a main ripple of extinction.

And the lexicon of wilds went on
nixing its descriptions. Slimming
the ancient index of references

for what is untamed, poisonous, and gorgeous—

ARTIFACTS

MYTHOS

SEEDS OF ELEUSIS

Persephone pressed her hands against the red film of the inside of a pomegranate seed. She was trapped. Under Hades' black dome, Persephone was not yet the chthonic goddess of spring. Her mother Demeter was getting wasted off fermented honey somewhere above ground, mourning her daughter's disappearance. A psychedelic search party raged for centuries; there was blood sacrifice, libations, methodical washings, and the dreams of animals projected on a big screen. Persephone eventually resurfaced—ran back to the warmth of

the world: elated, raped, with an expiration date of September. In her absence, the fields spidered with drought; now they blushed to hold her. These same glyphs of love and grief still murmur on a runestone—the myth of Demeter's daughter descending into soil. Myth of two flowers, rising like twin loons from a dark river. How Demeter did it—summoned Persephone and spring—is unknown. Only one line of the mystery survived. It says, simply, *an ear of grain cut in silence.* Other details of the rituals were sworn to secrecy, never spoken—except for one instance, when a cloud of bees seeped from a blue mouth.

PROPOLIS: GUMMY, MADE FOR SEALING CREVICES

and old as honey. Estuaries ran
between each hexadic peg, tessellating
in a beehive.
Good.
Gynecological. Pliable. Cement.
For the larynx,
for treat. Meant for
burns and ulcers. Good to
cauterize combs, this sterile resin
of alder, and poplar, and conifer, and beech,
and willow, and birch, and all the strong
words in poems, smeared on the mandible of a bee.

PROPOLIS: RUBBED FROM SPIKED THIGHS, BOUNDED INTO WAX

caskets for tiny lizards, beetles who made the wrong turn, and
other invaders, spun by bees in a funeral garb called propolis.
To smother out germs, rival breath, moisture and
light.

The Egyptians knew.

Propolis was our first embalmer.
Our final promise—to seal a dark cathedral
in the form of a body, shut
as a wintering hive.

Promise of—
we hope this works.

Promise of—
rest,
and we will snuff out the sun

THE WASP

I was about nine. The counselor passed out some juice. I sat on a wooden bench; I swung my knobby legs. The sun was a white blister. The heat asked hard questions and I kept saying I didn't know. On the stage there was a play about camp rules. The YMCA seemed desperate for a scrap of my attention. The wasp embedded in the bench had six legs and a narrow, aerodynamic waist. I sat in its territory. I ate a kind of cracker, sipped some sugary liquid. I thought of my mother. I screamed—not because I was leaving her, but because I wanted to be by myself; the camp environment was teeming with insects. The entire audience wiped their hands on their shorts. The counselor took my wrappers. The wasp chose the baby skin on the back of my knee. I felt its spindly body wiggling inside the crook. Someone stole me. I went to the nurse's RV, there was air conditioning, murmuring, and a mound of fluid forming. It was like the whole world happened to me.

SHAHRAZAD AND THE KING AT BRUNCH

(fragments from *The Thousand and One Nights*)

I.

Shahrazad, sharpened,
enters the night before her scheduled
death, and runs with it.

To set the King dreaming,
exquisite words open.

Syrian apples.
Osmani quinces, peaches from Uman, Jasmine of Aleppo

Cucumber from the Nile, limes from Egypt
Blood-red anemones, violets, pomegranate bloom

Sugar tarts with butter, velvet pastries
Sabuniyah biscuits, little cakes, lime tarts

Wrapped in banana leaves,
an almond—

II.

The King learns what it feels like to beg.
It's the one about the chef
famous for his *fesenjan*—chicken simmered
in spiced pomegranate syrup.

Secretly, the ending is this: *Two viziers beat him,*
broke his dishes and ruined his shop, all because
the meal had no kick to it. But Shahrazad keeps
that last part to herself. Instead, she

averts her black eyes. Counts the thousand
black seeds on a sweetened dough ball.
Sips orange blossom water and twists
her silent pinky on the sticky lip of a jar

of honey. She imagines the color of honey
is so sexy—lit from within—it could kill
at least two villages, every man in it, along with
every animal he ever loved or owned. So

Shahrazad, a literal hostage, goes to work
writing a legend in her head—when

it's still too early to speak.

III.

Come, sunrise.

Abundant verses,
like high-hanging

fruit, dangled
from a cliff, and

sure enough,
the dawn scaled

the King rejoiced
—*You!*

Stay,
darling

IV.

Atop a jeweled balcony, loose-growing jasmine canopy. Desert rose clusters
at every corner. Panorama featuring date palms and distant saltbush.
Juniper trees like upturned wrists steadying a ceiling.

The two of them, deeply unequal, share sunflower seeds,
poached eggs in yogurt, cracked pistachios piled on plinths,
pine nuts over lemon-honeyed halloumi, some royal

jelly. Vanilla labneh. Creamy vanilla rice tanned by cinnamon
and pricey maroon molasses. A slice of light
wrinkles across the table and stuns the small

flesh of pomegranate seeds glinting on a tray
like spare rubies. The King demands

an ending. Then
he lobs a platter at the wall.

Something soaked in yolk
slides. The yolk

disassembling, this is
the astonished morning.

V.

Centuries in the future, a Bedouin
walks into the Arabian desert. He is greeted by
2,200 species of acacia flowers, with
caves stuck on their branches. Not starving,
just empty in a morning way, the Bedouin
unpockets his jambiya digger and scrapes raw gold
dew from its crude wax cave and into the sunlight,
into a discarded plastic water bottle, living
to see another day in the land of honey.

NATURE POEM

For a while they considered Linnaeus
great Swiss biologist, Pornographer of Plants.
He's the guy responsible for the *or*
between flora or fauna. For drawing lines
in the sand—sand, which is neither
plant nor animal, just granular sea cliff shavings
of miscellaneous origin, sometimes shit out by parrotfish
who chew rocks with their vaguely human teeth and skim
the bottom of the ocean, which often recedes, revealing
its bald secrets. Linnaeus the Pornographer because
he looked mainly at mammalian breasts and floral testicles
to determine how conscious a thing is and under whose
kingdom it lives. People couldn't handle his peeping—at the pistil,
the pollen sac, the sticky knob of the stigma, which, I'll be
damned, is an actual term associated with the sex lives of flowers.

EARLIEST EVIDENCE

or, Rock Art at Araña Caves

The cave dragged darkness until it could no more,
and rushlight bloomed from a reed impregnated with grease.
An archivist took shape—
orator for the babbling children behind him.
He squatted, naked under a low ceiling.
Wet rockface swallowed iotas of fire that floated
up from his one particular palm.

Behold the earliest evidence of sweetness:
Slow and gold—it was the opposite of
marrow—a full-bodied taste not sucked from a kill
or buttery like bones. Pressed this rumor into stone. Someone
gnashed soot and charcoal into shadows until
there came a chorus of bees.

In the painting, a cave man swings his basket
full of pillaged honey. His flat body peers into
an actual hole in the wall—a limestone chunk
missing from a valley near the Escalona River.
The hole is the opening to a hive.
The caveman climbs a ladder of liana vines—not the name
for a species, but for the habit of growing vertically—and
licks his whole hand. The swarm of bees

is a smudge of pigment. Color of crushed berries,
red ochre, spit, and flower brains. The bees
are mute as confetti, blown from their hive
for eternity. Until someone finally
gasps. Someone finally
covers their mouth, and just touches.

INSATIABLE

or, Recipe for Last Supper

chicory root plucked
from a tuberous sleeve in earth,
dusted, bagged, and hoisted
onto a wood cart, clipped to a divine
mule heaving its barreled chest
through Jerusalem city streets, sweat
beading quietly in its soft hide, not
crushed by the linen sacks on its back
which are full of bitter herbs, celery, coriander,
beetroot. A head of lettuce bounces on a bump
and rolls to the feet of a beggar, then
rolls to the feet of the king of man, seated with
arms agape, whose very presence at this
bountiful spread suggests that spiced nuts
churned to charoset, the velvet of a bean
stew, fresh-slain rack of ribs, side of
steaming fish sauce and dates that
cleave in his mouth, unleavened bread, aromatized
wine, is heaven, is the shadow of death
not yet a thing, is the taste of all that is good
filling the throats of sheep, is the lamb of
god sucking an olive, preparing
the words, *I thirst.*

A DREAM IN WHICH I AM EVE, EXITING

I.

Enter: God, wondering why you're so naked, and why your boyfriend, Chadam (preferred name Chad), looks like he just saw a ghost. *You ate from the tree didn't you. I specifically asked you not to eat from the tree. It was the one thing I asked you not to do.*

A wasp tries to leave early, but she's stuck in the goo.

II.

(This is the design, though. The wasp is supposed to get stuck in the fig. Every fig has or has had at least one wasp inside it, burrowing a tunnel, boring its way to the center, watched by an audience of a thousand seedlings the size of pinheads. The wasp is digging towards the inside flower—a system of glands and petals tucked in

the warm nursery of the fig's green husk. Her mission is twofold: pollinate, and birth. She crawls inside. She lays her eggs and kicks off the pollen stuck to her legs. She loses an antenna, her wings fall away, she remains a forward-moving body pushing through the pulp.

She is rewarded with slumber in the tight bed of a fig [mankind will never know this kind of sleep]. Then, in exchange for the life of a wasp, the flesh of the fig purples around it, sweetening.

This classic combination—of noble instinct, crappy destiny, and unsung martyrdom—dangles from a twig on the wind. Right above where you and a very nude Chad are lounging.)

III.

And the fruit that catches your forbidden eye? The fig. The fruit that
is not a fruit but a flower in reverse. The fruit that clutches its own
flower like a breath. The fruit that will turn the color of a storm as
it matures; the fruit that eats wasps; the kind of fruit that wasps
dream of dying inside of. That's the one. That's the fruit for you.
Coincidence?

Chad, beautiful and dumb, missing a rib but otherwise has it all,
looks like he's noticing you for the first time. Then he slaps a gnat
that dared land on his pectoral, and looks into his own hand.

IV.

They'll talk about this moment *ad infinitum*—but they'll say it was a red, terrible apple.

It just so happens that in Latin the word for evil sounds the same as the word for apple — *malum et malum* — unrelatedly. So the writers take creative license. They tweak the story to change the exact species of ignominy. Not because you—*oops!*—ate the wrong fruit. But because everyone loves a pun that reinforces what they already know. A play on words that seals the ending in an airtight container.

And because, this way, even if God forgot to make those tiny, incredible fig wasps, you would still be lured by that thing in the distance.

Because apple blossoms are a lot less complicated. Because God designed honeybees, not wasps, as the chief accomplice to apples. (Semantics.)

V.

Here comes God making his way through the tropical thicket. You swallow, grab a bunch of fig leaves, and thrust them over yours and Chad's *mons pubis*. Chad says Jesus Christ Eve this is like sandpaper. You say please don't. He says you couldn't have picked another leaf? You say these are the only leaves in paradise. He says right. You say you're free to go out and find a softer, smoother leaf to cradle your privates while I tackle the bigger problem. Meanwhile, shame—like an audience of a thousand seeds the size of pinheads—gathers round your body with individual bags of popcorn.

VI.

You are full of fig, and the fig is full of the memory of a wasp, you digesting the fig, the fig absorbing the wasp, both processes made possible by your God-given enzymes, every inch of this scenario designed to trap you in its delicious, sticky center. Listen, if we're talking about the dawn of Western time, you're always the bad guy. You're always in an itchy loin cloth begging for mercy in the next millennia. Trying to fit that little leaf over the ugly bulk of original sin while Chad gladly points the finger. Of a snake. At you. Unless—

EINSTEIN TO VIRGIL

(on species extinction)

Four years? Supposedly a death sentence
for mankind without insects. It's not
my own genius I'm questioning, but the soundbite.
I never said it. The statistic became common
knowledge for better or for worse. Then,
the statistic being authorless also became a well-known
fact. Listen—a prediction like that is its own
mother—i.e., naturally occurring. At least the drama
was a little fiery under the ass of humanity
for a short while. Before the fact cooled. And
hardened. And turned into an enormous sheet of glass,
like a window, disguised as the sky,
tricking pigeons to fly through.

VIRGIL TO EINSTEIN

(offering the quaint medieval tradition, *bugonia*)

Have you tried considering the issue in reverse?
Instead of one extinction leading to another,
my vision of bees, their ambition, is rosier. Almost
heroic. Not exactly optimism, but *ox-born*.

Kill a 33-month-old ox in Spring, I told them,
without mercy (I cannot write it here),
inside a small clay hut. Smooth over
the windows, the orifices (stay with me) with mud,

rosemary, fine linen, and thyme. Block wind
at all costs. Leave a little air. Leave
for three weeks. Return to let the light in, and find
the ox is huge, gone, and a hive. The hut

alive with bees and
all proof of metamorphosis enclosed
in a single black hair. Or
simply bury

the carcass underground. Let only the horns
irrupt from the quiet dirt. Give the horns ample time
to think about what they've done, and out
(I assure you) will come numberless bees.

What I mean to say is, the soul of an ox transforms
into a swarm of bees to atone for its life
spent ravaging our verdant earth. The bees
burst forth, victorious and thick as raindrops
in a summer cloud.

I call the whole thing *warm humor*, not
to give irony all the power.
The flower-sucking bees
grow up, despite their parent, in bodies
so tender to the fields they sleep
curled up on weeds.

And justice—pure and sourceless—goes on
fermenting inside the soft bones of the ox.

Not bad, right?

FLORA

CAROLYN'S ORCHIDS

The only person I know
who can keep an orchid
alive is a poet who flung
herself into the middle of
a civil war in El Salvador
in the '70s, and got incredibly
famous for a poem about
a colonel decimating his people's
kneecaps and taking human
rights very lightly. In fact,
he terrorized her by tossing
a dried ear from a bag into
her glass of wine, I think. No.
It was only a cup of water.
She also reported that girls
were sexually mutilated.
She says that she and I share
an interest in bees. She has
a poem about beehive graves,
mounds entombing the dead in
ancient Greece; for this reason
I've seen her name appear next to
Agamemnon's, but also Pablo
Neruda's, André Breton's, and
other poets who have dared more
than I. I wonder, though, do I
really have to do all that, just to keep
my orchids alive?

PERSIMMON

A stranger asked in Korean, *you try?*
My family had recently become three oceans
away. There are different kinds of persimmon;
some chop hard and sound like solid wood.
But this first stranger, she passed me
a fruit full of dimples.

MEMORY OF MOUNT EXMOOR, ENGLAND

Wrapped in your ugly wool-collar canvas coat,
I could barely see you—but I remember squinting
at that curling tuft of black hair, subsuming the whole
white ball behind you. Over-exposed, you near-
ly burned in tidal waves of yellow hay, slow-swaying
around your long legs, your distant body backlit by
a white sky. You were in the middle,
right in front of the sun, and pulling me towards

MOON GARDEN

plume of a rose
iceberg, spoon
of a calla lily,
mugwort by day
is artemisia by night,
euonymus foliage and
azalea hair, lunar as
the deep white navel of
datura weeping, unfurling
cigarettes, glow, rhododendron
bosom, phlox creeping starlit,
and occasionally a stampede
of lamb's ear silvering, underfoot

CASHEW

the shoe that droops from a
pulpy red flower, a kidney-
shaped boxing glove splitting
to cradles, like two small
gondolas in the great
hulls of my father's hands

RIND

or, *Still Life with Lobster* by Joris van Son, 1660

But first, a lemon, ribboning
in a way that cannot be accidental.
The pocked rind spiraling, shaving itself
down to the neon pulp now nakedly
a wheel. The lemon pirouettes
from its skin—a toy of gravity.
Such choreography of the peel
is impossible, is the fantasy of
my bitterness, asking to be chewed.

PORTRAIT OF SPRING

or, *Vertumnus* by Giuseppe Arcimboldo, 1590

Pupils like black cherries.
Mustache made of dueling hazelnuts.
Upper eyelids, two boomerangs of snow pea pods.
A few strewn shallots for the under-eye bags, and Spring,
your nose, pinched at the top, ballooning at the end, is a pear.
Eyebrows like wheat blown east and west. Elsewhere wheat is
poking from around your head in the fashion of a periscope, or
sparks. Your two hard cheeks like McIntosh apples shined and almost
red. A couple of strawberry butts populate your bottom lip, and your dark ringed
hair is a mess of concord grapes, strands of plump globes of blue juice, not quite
the length of your face. Finished with a green furred chestnut for the little mound
of chin. Your prickling beard is a bouquet of seeds. All this atop your thick stalk of
a neck, muscled gourd of chest, feathered, fainting, rippling how pulled sheets of
cabbage do, and your Adam's apple not round, but jagged as a pulled turnip
whose electric roots clamor back towards sleep.

THIS IS NOT ABOUT US (IT'S JUST ABOUT DESIRE AND THE PLAGUE)

More than a crisis, a phenomenon is how
scholars describe the bubonic
craze that made the Dutch
desire, more than
anything, a tulip

There were flower auctions and
commissioned portraits of bulbs,
certain bulbs worth thousands of seventeenth-century coins

Bulb-like symptoms
developed in certain parts of the body,
round nodules in the armpits or groin, for example, but also
intolerance to light, pain in the back and limbs,
sleeplessness, apathy, and delirium—

But in this version of modernity,
in the floral department
of Trader Joe's, I keep
my hands, my saliva, and
this bit of trivia to myself

Because we are running out of money
and because your mind needs a speedometer,
I want to say, *you look pretty even in a mask
tightened by safety pins in the back of your head*

To purchase means to buy, or
to get a grip on—to want to consume—

Tulpenmanie. They say it was like
a fever inside
an era of fever—

I want to tell you, but you've gone
worrying down some other aisle. And I am pushing
a shopping cart of baby's breath, the color of plums

SPECULATION (IT'S JUST ABOUT DESIRE AND THE PLAGUE)

But wait. The irony goes deeper. A luxury bulb was a broken one.
What causes a tulip to break? stayed a question
until several mutations later. Petals
streaked in crimson and bleach white.
Hypnotic as a riddle, symmetrical as arson
—alien,
two cupped leaves splitting to birth its singular holy orb.

Chimneysweeps, nobles, maidservants, and Rembrandt all
froze in the glow of a tulip.
In 1636, the cost of a single ruined bloom
was the same as a mansion on the canal.
The most irreparable flowers were hoarded by one
especially bewitched collector who
considered this prismatic miracle
private. Prices surged. Then
burst. After the market crashed, broken tulips were
outlawed across the Netherlands, and Amsterdam's out-
skirts wilted, dense with orphaned bulbs whose
bright little heads
bobbed and bobbed in the fields—

Speaking from the future, we know a seed only breaks
from a virus, which usually sends flowers deathward, but
a tulip swallows
and becomes it. So a plague upon plants
caused a plague of want for color, in the wake
of a black plague upon man.
This was a time when
you could put a diseased thing in the ground
and watch it eclipse an inheritance.
This was a time when

rosacca bloomed in cheeks,
and bones seemed whiter than usual.

FAUNA

COLONY COLLAPSE

Since we're on the topic of Europe and
symptoms, this seems like a good time
to mention colony collapse. Signs to look for:
abnormal brood pattern, sunken or chewed combs.
Larvae slumped to the side of their chambers. Worst is
supersedure of the Queen. The cause is
usually a parasite. The parasite only affects
European honeybees, which, as we know, were
brought to America by Columbus and kept on bee farms
primarily for the purpose of wax candles. When they escaped
into the wild, where they subsequently built little monarchies,
colonists referred to them as feral. Of course, Puritan missionaries invented
the idea that Native Americans didn't even have a word for bee. Wrong.
There were 4,000 thriving species of "feral bees" at the time when
the Mayflower et al. docked and unloaded its many treasures.
Colony collapse is a spore that ripples towards crops and
people and their money. Notably it's never been found in the beehives
of native populations, which is a joke of decent design.

BEES REBRAND

Why colony? Don't you think
we're past that now?
Why not a post-structural
orchestra, or a type of sky?

MID-SWIG

I read that a woman who was living in the same mountains as me, was in her robe,
drinking coffee. A bear was halfway in her living room. His other half
was starved, and still on the porch. The morning light twitched on the rim
of his bear nostrils and before she could scream, the bear
wrapped his black lips around a hummingbird
feeder that the woman curiously kept inside. She said
her cat loves to sip puddles after it rains, so she
left the screen door open. With its mauve tongue,
the bear blotted some birdseed and chased
it down with simple syrup. The coffee mug shattered. Now the bear
was completely unaware he was in the same living room where
my neighbor watches *Good Morning America*. He entered the house
the same way a hand enters a mailbox, or a hand
theorizes the pros and cons of swiping an anthill. *Heads up:*
they're getting bolder, she posted, along with a photo
of the bear holding the hummingbird
feeder from its paw, looking oddly like a grown man
in an empty bar, mid-swig of a pint of beer. I always feel deflated
when I read these things, because I think, *where is my*
bear? Why not me?

BEES DANCE

"In this manner, *Apis florea* confirms our long-cherished suspicion that dance on a horizontal surface with orientation directly according to the sky, represents the more ancient form in which direction was indicated."—Karl von Frisch, ethologist

Somewhere a bee is dancing
in total darkness, to a viewership of sixty thousand
other, comprehending bees
who watch, listen for her instructions, towards
the opposite of hunger—

—Listen, if I had rhythm
if I could trace the shape of
a nectarine in the clouds,
if I could use the earth's magnetic field
to pinpoint the precise
zenith of my desire, and if
I could tell you how
to get there, I would

THE FIRST TIME WE WENT SWIMMING

—Come on.

Nothing lives in it. The quarry
is the residue of dynamite. Man-made
and barren. There's no fish or
food chain that human bodies
only briefly interrupt.

The quarry yawned
at your hypothesis, unbothered by
the speck of you—tiny blip
on a blue radar,
talking at the sky.

You were so shiny.
You were shiny from the inside,
enjoying a moment of total buoyancy,
quartz in your eyelashes,
and a shark's smile.

Oh,
the first time we went swimming,
I was swimming

BEE-EATER

The sound *distinctive, mellow, liquid*
The babies *blind, helpless, bald*
Of the order *passerine*, from the Latin
passer, which caused the name *sparrow*,
because of the word *through*, and *song*

In any case, nobody really painted
the bee-eater bird. Except for two choice instances—
one has blue cheeks, gold plumage, in the rubble of a Roman villa.
The other is green and carmine in a mural inside Queen Hatshepsut's
tomb. Luckily, bee-eaters still nest in dunes, lay glossy eggs,
and emit their sweet high trill. Aristotle voted to
kill them. Virgil agreed—to protect the hives

from the bee eater's venom-soaked tongues.
They plot against insects, falcons, whip
snakes, and any red fox
whiskering the edge of an egg.
In flight, they appear as Vishnu's bow—
the arc of the beak, exquisite and crisp
as the black bar marking
this bird's small face,
swelling in the eye of a dingo.

Once upon a time, charred bee-eater toes
made medicinal smoke. And the salve of their fat
repelled biting flies. Even flies remember
the scent of archer gods, and the war
cry of a bee-eater.

ANIMALS

I slip the dog a trachea
dipped in honey, freeze-dried, and stolen
from an already-beef cow.
The guilt is there, but managed,
manufactured by a major retail chain
the dog doesn't care
to know the name of. She—sometimes
my singular purpose—licks her gleaming
chops and lets the whites of her eyes disappear
at the idea of this honeyed organ
passing from a bag to her mouth.

We usually pause here,
right before the transaction. To adore
each other. To prove we aren't wolves.

To miss our chance
to ask, *so, what is your real name?*

8 PM IN BROOKLYN, JULY 2020

O how we leaned from balconies.

how the bees turned over in their cells.

how we cheered & prayed & whooped. how
we hollered with our good lungs, how we
waved and spun in place. how
we stuck our torsos out
of the enormous pores of skyscrapers
to applaud the dying nurses. to scatter
a trail of breadcrumbs. to blow

our kisses. to be a
little like wind.

DECRESCENDO

End
at the place where the sound gets in.
Sweep across my cheek skin. Startle me
with the short gust of your thumb
across the carved shell of my ear—the sound
of a tiny explosion
in slow motion, or a swarm approaching
and passing, right in front of my face.
You lay there, sort of dreaming.

TERRA

QUEER APPALACHIA

Take me to the holler.
I want to see the cows
Big Mamaw's grave and
something about tobacco fields.

I don't recall all you said at Barley's, but you
introduced yourself with an anecdote
about toothbrushes made from
chewed-up willow branches and
coyotes loping along a
wooded backyard—Uncle Clark's
and Aunt Zella's. Big Mamaw called you
Little Tweeter and threw
pollywogs in the air.
Did you know
in academia, everyone's talking
about queer Appalachia?
And "statistically unlikely" is your best angle.
You tug on all-purpose bootstraps
under the table, ready to dazzle

me with the story. *I was baptized*
on the side of the road in a concrete basin.
Farmers dressed in diaphanous curtains dunked me
till I saw God. One time my parents
decided to be American
traveling gospel singers, ripping me
out of a one-room schoolhouse to staple
shag carpet to the metal walls
of the bus we lived in.
Coach, maybe, was the only gay woman
I knew, and she's still married to
Earl. Take me to the holler.

It just so happens that night you dragged an opossum
out of the road. Not quite dead—in a poem
I wrote that its life "teetered on the cusp
of the longest, bluest hour." I was knee-deep

in Maggie Nelson, queen of the queers.
Queen of blue,
I told you. *Who?*

OK, take me to the Cumberland River
where the cows pose and the ghost of Big Mamaw croons.
Did you know
Judith Butler is actually very attractive?
Who is Judith Butler? You haul a kayak
over your rippling bulk of a shoulder and
set us going down the river.

Kudzu vines dip beneath the tree line like ropes.
Southern gothic.
The river ends in a pool of long, thin men.
Wading.
Their ponytails whip
out of the water and we dock. I hadn't noticed
the weather is hot.
Even the buzzards stop and reconsider.
And the current
carries a fleet of crinkled beer cans

toward us. Did they see
you kiss me?
I don't think I've ever seen a real gun in my life.
How fast can I load a boat?
I ask myself while you take us out,
you rush to take us out—
to take my dumb ass out of the holler.

SHORT LECTURE ON WART CURE

Hard to believe your mother dropped you
on the doorstep of a milky-eyed sorceress

in the woods. You didn't go inside, just stood there,
three feet tall on her porch. She pressed her long fingers—

white as cream, arthritic as a black gum tree blown
bare—to the warts growing callus on your wrist.

You said the witch stared into your pupils, then
that was it. I said, *you don't think*

it was maybe, like, frankincense, or tea tree oil?
Lots of different reasons why that could happen

just by touching you. You say I'm free
to conjecture, but it's just hill people stuff.

BEELINE

I.

There was a struggle on Old Hardy Road. It goes—

The Billiter woman in her garden
cleans out a bird bath and dumps a fountain
shaped like the Angel Gabriel—its stagnant bowl
of water, bacteria and moss—out on the ground.

Known to destroy toys that fall in her yard, she once
broke a doll whose little finger was on her property line.
She chucked your dad's and his twin brother's train set
in the river behind her house.

Ms. Billiter knew everyone in Toler. Except for
the teenager behind her. A sudden shadow in her garden.

What happens next makes hares stand up in the fields,
makes blackbirds lift from the tops of buckeye trees.

II.

When your dad was a kid, he and his twin brother
walked home from school, past the train tracks
and Pond's Creek. There was the usual echo of
a pebble skipping down the road, otherwise

silent. Toler is not actually a place that tolls—not like
a toller dog calls to a dead pheasant in a field. Rather
Toler is a place where the alphabet gets away
with almost anything. There's Kentucky

woodlands, brackish tidal marshes. When you tell me this story,
there's the bridge and the high beam where you used to balance
towards the Dairy Queen. The Daniel Boone Forest watching

over your father's boyhood. And everything
brick and mortar peeks from a maze of crabgrass.

III.

Two black snakes lie nose-to-nose on the train tracks.

Your dad and his twin crouched down to look at them,
parallel on railroad ties. Not moving, their snake eyelids

peeled back. *Weird*, the twins thought, and kept walking
towards the mouth of the holler, thinking of
home. What they didn't see

was the throng of cop cars surfing
the long stretch of tar. Sirens vibrate
all four eardrums of the boys, now on edge.

IV.

Before anyone can clock it, a sinewy, denim-clad
teenager rips off Highway 119, a rifle over his shoulder, and his
other shoulder, newly pubescent, pumps his body up the hill.
The boy's sandy hair flames behind him.

What in the hell, the twins are too young to say.
The whole scene

is framed by Kentucky's chokeberry trees and other
deep rooted species. The teenager eyes a dark direction
that might welcome him
and dives headfirst into the brush.

V.

The twins made it to the top of the hill where
two cop cars parked nose-to-nose, blocking
the street. How could they not rise on their toes
to peer over the hood of the car's
white lip? Look at

the Billiter woman, dead on the street. Wild grass
creeps around her, each weed the entrail of a root in
a national forest. In Toler, several life cycles pass

and nobody questions the kids, now
adults, despite what they've seen.
You say, *the killer made a beeline
into the mountains.* I say the phrase
doesn't tell us anything. You say chatter
runs under the seams of Toler like
a church bell keeps on ringing,
full of ends.

UPON ARRIVING AT GREAT-AUNT DOROTHY'S FUNERAL

You took me to the spot where your mother buried her
Barbies. Where the Tug Fork let himself in twice and rushed
at Williamson County. You told me how your aunt sang with
Dolly, how the flood robbed generations blind and drowned
birds and coal miners in their own hills, how dirty water churned
into moonshine. Wild onion grass, orphan microwaves, and lop-
sided school buses sprouted from the damp curb. We arrived
at the church. It was full of relatives who left. They still call you
your deadname. In their accent, we barely recognize it—like *Lorn*, e.g.,
this is forlorn. Well. Dorothy's funeral was your most handsome
day. Hair slicked back, clear frames, your kimono-style jacket,
and Yves Saint Laurent shoes. Mud seeped up from the
parking lot. Every Christmas, your fifty-year-old mother
asks for a Holiday Barbie, and Williamson County asks for
the return of Virginia bluebells. Your whole family was there.
You know, the way rain gathers in a footprint.

THESE DAYS WE IMAGINE GETTING A GUN

I imagine the barrel is greasy. I imagine your smile erases facts that I don't like. Such as—you know how to hold a weapon, and teeth are just exposed bones. A few weeks ago, the neighbor called out, *y'all sisters?* and we obviously said yes. It's not that bad—I used to live next door to a man with a manifesto tattooed on his scalp. His windows were patched with duct tape and plastic camouflage tarp, and the bumper sticker on his family minivan said *No Fags*. I imagine I was scared. Then, I imagine you in bed—your skin is the bright shade of a tooth, or the meniscus of milk when it touches the glass edge of a cup and turns a little blue. A magnolia at night. You told me you learned when you were young.

OUT IN YOUR COUNTRY

I.

Before the options became limited, you didn't know what I meant by *drive*. My parents often used to *take a drive*. I have no idea where they went (the children weren't invited) but my best guess is, my mother and father disappeared to ogle the exteriors of other people's houses. Anyway, I suggested we take a drive because: what else were we going to do? *You just go in one direction and see where you end up—*

I grew up on Long Island. And now I hate the beach, but I love the feeling of an edge. I understand not everybody feels this way about edges. You certainly don't. But you're driving. To find an edge and let me kiss it.

We landed way out "in the country." No trespassing. No fire stations. Nowhere to hide. A humongous maple tree explodes from a hole in the side of an old silo. You point at quilts, the diamond patterns, their immunity to rain. A shack with a tin roof and other doomsday-type places whir past in the window. The fields roll themselves open. And the hills bounce, voluptuous. Mocking the sky.

II.

The dog is dying to get out of the backseat while chickens cross the road. The chickens go quick, not thinking of their inevitable slaughter, just escaping for the sake of escape. The cows ruminate on several world-changing ideas, none of which have to do with meat, their own or anyone else's. Cows use the word *ruminate* to describe chewing cud. Humans took it to describe thinking— chewing with our minds.

O'Hara wrote odes about the countryside.

And the day came fat with an apple in its mouth.

The whole pasture looked like our meal.

But you orphaned this breed of nothing a long time ago. Because your mohawk faces out the window and some of your freshly buzzed hair is in my mouth. And you *ruminate* aloud about if your Honda Fit looks a certain way—whatever that means.

You ask me where to go: *Left or right? Which road looks more harrowing?*

You mean because we're gay. Animals. You're talking about the edge.

Look—nothing happens on this drive, nobody gets hurt. But I realize I'll never be inside this valley deep enough not to see it so brightly. My sense of safari will pretty much eat anything.

III.

I want to see more of the barbed wire. The gray barns all loaded
with ghosts. An ax fighting with a piece of wood, a lone figure
swinging an ax in a side yard. A wide rushing creek cracks open the
land—the water a gloss of sparkles over white limestone shards.
It's the sort of creek where someone would remember someone
else drowning. Maybe from childhood. A someone who gets
remembered in a song.

You say nobody around here writes a will, but there are funeral
auctions where precious family heirlooms are silently bid on by the
public. Where unmarked cardboard boxes are carted off by
strangers, and buried deeper in, or shuttled out of, this part of the
country.

Dumbly, I say, *do you think that's more like graverobbing,
or beachcombing?*

You couldn't afford any of Big Mamaw's old stuff. She was another
one without a will—because *hell if Mamaw had a lawyer.* What I'm
trying to say is, sometimes it feels like you give me this place for free.

IV.

Reminds you of the .45 your dad wore on his belt all through Christmas dinner. Reeks of your roadside baptism, the strange shape of the concrete basin that swallowed your sins and coughed up me. This heat. This thrill, thirty years later.

I once read: *Poems flooded me. They fell on me like wild bees.*

I tell you that the image of the bees is about being devoured by the thing you love the most. I know we aren't safe out here but at least we're full of words. I am talking about the sublime. I think.

It turns out: The Polish poet who penned that line was phoning in from occupied Poland, 1940-something.

She also said, in a separate book, *I have no talent*, as if poems like hers were not light. As if poets were pools of water—just refracting what they steal. As if light could be pillaged from the atmosphere. As if a poem is what's at the bottom of a bunch of bees and I'm scrambling to grab it. To take it with me, to remember this drive in your country.

V.

So—what does it mean: that I take joy in this kind of drive, dreaming my way through. To think I even know what it means to need to drive or to need to dream of deliberate peril, especially when the options seem limited, peril being something to do—

The drive is over.

We leave because we're kissing.

We kiss because we're leaving.

ETHOS

COME SLOWLY—EDEN! (AFTER EMILY DICKINSON)

Sure, suppose Eden emerges
slowly. And suppose the lucky bee
feigns bashfulness. He approaches
a Jessamine flower so very gold, golder
than her hovering suitor. This
beauty queen, this trumpet vine
reclines across the banks and slopes,
horizontal and unsupervised.
(Right—I'm following.) Then

Dickinson's bee refers to his tube-like mouth
as a pair of "unused lips" and purses them.
Black chamber of the bloom
is slightly ajar. He hums around it
and pretends to faint. The sun appears briefly
as a puddle of sugar. He enters, sips and—
Dickinson reports—sinks
to the bottom of her small pond.
(Well. I'm sure some version of that happened.)
Meanwhile critics—let's call them Dickinists—mourn
this poor male bee, subsumed by
feminine mystique. (Okay. Look.
Dickinson is asleep

in her grave. Do we honestly believe she and her genius
forwent the scientific fact that almost every insect
is a woman insect? And only a few drone bees are male?
A drone leaves the hive once in his life. To lay down
with his ruler and promptly perish, his precious cargo
parked indefinitely in the abdomen of a queen. Point being
a lady Jessamine would never meet a drone—only
another timid, winged, seraphim. Suppose

there's no secrets between a bee and her flowers. Suppose
there is some benefit to the nearsightedness of a poet.
Suppose Dickinson was free to write a hundred poems
about honeybees masquerading as lovers, lovers

masquerading as bees masquerading as Dickinson and
humming in a world of hushed feelings. If you ask me,
she was teetering on the edge of a petal, wanting
to get lost in the balms.)

THE BOTANICAL TRADITION

This much is true.
No male bee ever meets a flower
let alone kisses her. That means

This is a pair of wives.
They see each other through a dark keyhole
across a perfect line of sight.
Nothing else.
There is no other possible direction.
These two are wedded.
The story isn't timeless. But it is
archaic—full of again, and again, and again.

One is circadian in her rhythms.
One has eyes that sleep watching the sun.
One is called the wrong name.
One is interpreted and remade.
Their dynamic is chronicled.
They are resurrected and eulogized and
immortalized in odes under the wrong names.
They recognize each other.
They love so good, the arrangement lives for eons, feeding itself.
They love under open clouds.
They crane their soft necks on the wind.

One cannot see herself.
One sees an ultraviolet lake where the grass should be.
They tell each other how to go.
Some days they're so busy.
Some days they swear to meet in a midnight valley.
Some days they swear to meet in the deep groove of habit.

LITTLE BOY, THERE ARE NO ROSES
IN THIS POEM

for LJ

To put it in terms I can understand,
you lean on the word *buds*—as in, rose buds.
To disguise the poem I ask you to write, you title it

Thelarche. At first, I think it's a kind of bug. Or maybe
a moon's first name. Greek and obscure.
I don't know. You're smarter than me.

Turns out thelarche is more sinister—budding, as in,
a speeding train. Budding as in, Salvation
Army t-shirts, huge and shapeless as
a sudden flood. Budding

as in, *Little boy! Stop grabbing my peaches!* as in
the shrill old man who launched frog-like
from his porch and chased the back of
your blonde head through miles of budding
orchards. To avenge his family fruits. To teach
a younger man a lesson.

Well. You were hopping fences in Kentucky.
And he was a furious gardener. But also
the first stranger to ever call you the right thing, as in—
a boy. As if—that was all it took

to be seen:
sneak into the wrong yard, at the wrong biological time,
at the right distance, and just try, try,
to steal for yourself the juicy world
of a peach.

THERE MIGHT BE ROSES IN THIS POEM

for LJ

It's the afternoon of the surgeon's call.
You are ecstatic and your ecstaticism
is mine. My response is missing
sentence structure, and is botanical in nature,
for some primordial knee-jerk reason.

I cut the heads off two roses
and float them in two wine tumblers of water.
I forget my map. I present these cocktails to you as a gift.
We don't own the glassware or the house or each other
so really, I give you this image and one interpretation—

How free the body of a rose is
when not balancing
on that plate-spinning stem.
Rose body buoyant as salt. Rose
body dense as a palmed
finch. Rose body just
a hypothesis—subject
to change, time, and other factors.

The cocktails are for me, too, maybe more
for me. I prefer to think of your blood
as floral and figurative than red
and spillable at the whims of a surgeon's
swift hands. Nonetheless we celebrate
the glory of medicine, being born
in this millennium and in a major city.
We picture those two stunning cuts
running parallel forever. Whatever we
exclaim or worry drops

to its knees before your futuristic,
flat, Roman bust. You kiss me. You kiss
you. Yes, there might be roses
in this poem, but thank god, they're the last ones.

LOVE POEM

I will tell you exactly how it is.
I don't need a cornfield
to comment on your blondeness, to tell you
about my cinematically sorry sense of direction,
which you already know, or to confess
that I am aimless, that I float leaf-like,
lazy and nostalgic. I get eggshellish
just thinking of you and I am running
through this poem blindfolded and screaming.
As if I could write it how it really is, as if I'm not
a scrap of amber paling in the bright October
of your hair.
You can wait in line for
saffron, for marigolds, for me to
get it right in one long verse, but I don't need
to metaphorize caramel, which is already
sugar when it's burning, and I don't need
a risqué simile about your legs, your
freakin' legs, designed by some cruel
yellow egret, hellbent on mocking my weakness.
I like to think I can write a poem whenever I want,
about whatever. I don't need my pervasively strange
love of your hair
to make this thing work.

BEES KNEES

And yet
Aren't we the best possible thing?

Our knees are the phrase for
so satisfied—we were never
meant to run. Instead, we fold
into our own bellies.
We lift like silver fumes

over the loam. We twist away
like a balloon released by a child, or like
a child released from a ballet.

The sky darkens with possibility.
Suddenly, I realize
there are many of us.

ACKNOWLEDGMENTS

A version of the "Prelude" poem, titled "Playing with Bees," was a winner of the 2023 Treehouse Climate Action Prize from the Academy of American Poets. It was published in *Poem-a-Day* on Poets.org.

"Little Boy, There Are No Roses in This Poem" was shortlisted for the 2023 Alpine Poetry Prize.

"Rind" and "Insatiable (Recipe for Last Supper)" were published in *AGNI* literary magazine (2023).

"The Botanical Tradition," "Come slowly—Eden!," and "Love Poem" were published in *Screen Door Review* (2023).

"Colony Collapse" and "Virgil to Einstein" appear in *The Decadent Review* (2023).

"A Dream in Which I am Eve, Exiting" was published in *NonBinary Review* (Zoetic Press, 2023).

"Bees Rebrand" was published in *Blue Unicorn* poetry journal (2023).

"This Is Not About Us (It's Just About Desire and the Plague)" appeared in *POETRY* magazine (October 2021) and was reprinted by *The Rising Phoenix Review* (2022).

"Queer Appalachia" appeared in *POETRY* magazine (October 2021) and was reprinted in *Dream of the River*, an LGBTQ anthology published by Jacar Press (2021), as well as *The Rising Phoenix Review* (2022).

A version of "Out in Your Country" is included in The Spring Creek Project's *The Nature of Isolation* poetry collection (2020) and in *Dream of the River* (2021).

A version of "8 pm in Brooklyn, July 2020" was published by *The Revolution (Relaunch)* newspaper in 2020.

The poem "Carolyn's Orchids" refers to the poem "The Colonel" (1978) by Carolyn Forché.

Two lines from Frank O'Hara's poem "Animals" (1950) appear in the prose poem "Out in Your Country."

"Bees Dance" includes a quote from Karl von Frisch's *The Dance Language and Orientation of Bees* (1967).

"Come slowly—Eden!" references the poem of the same name by Emily Dickinson (1860).

"Shahrazad and The King at Brunch" includes erasures from *The Thousand and One Nights*, edited by J. C. Mardrus and E. P. Mathers (1987).

RK Fauth earned a master's degree in English from Georgetown University, where she also served as a Lannan Poetry Fellow. Her writing has appeared in *POETRY* magazine, *Poem-a-Day*, *West Trade Review*, *The Decadent Review*, *AGNI* literary magazine, and elsewhere. Fauth has held fellowships and distinctions from the Fulbright Program, the Alpine Fellowship Foundation, the Lannan Foundation for Poetics and Social Practice, and the Academy of American Poets. She currently lives in Asheville, North Carolina.